A|973

# DEAN CLOSE SCHOOL

## LIBRARY

VERBUM DEI LUCERNA

This book must be returned by the latest date stamped below

© 1973 MICHAEL SULLIVAN

*Printed in Singapore*

ISBN 0 500 41050 X

# INTRODUCTION

This small book can give no more than a glimpse of what China has achieved in art and archaeology since the establishment of the People's Republic. Nearly all the works of art I have included were either discovered or first published after 1949, a substantial number having been unearthed since the beginning of the Cultural Revolution in 1966.

In 1948 the Kuomintang government had shipped to Taiwan the bulk of the huge Palace Museum collection, and it was widely thought abroad that under Communism China's cultural heritage would suffer, as had that of Soviet Russia after 1917, from sheer neglect – if it was not deliberately destroyed. But that did not happen. On the contrary, during the 1950s the decaying palaces in Peking and other important ancient monuments across the length and breadth of the country were restored and made accessible to the public, the Palace Museum was re-established and new provincial museums opened, while a national archaeological service was set up with a network of regional offices covering every province. At the same time the government launched an ambitious programme to educate the masses in the importance of preserving their heritage, which they were told had been created by their forbears and now belonged, at last, to all.

Fifteen years of archaeological work had already produced spectacular results when, in 1966, the storm of the Great Proletarian Cultural Revolution burst upon China. Basically the Cultural Revolution was an effort to root out old ideas and values, to break up the bureaucracy established by the Communist party, and to achieve a spiritual regeneration spearheaded by youth – the Red Guard. In their passionate and often uncontrolled hunt for vestiges of 'bourgeois' culture, the Red Guard certainly destroyed or removed some works of art and libraries, chiefly in private hands.

Images and tablets in Buddhist temples were papered over with Red Guard slogans, and in a few cases smashed. The museums quickly closed their doors, and in June 1966 publication of all the art and archaeology journals abruptly ceased. Once again, fears rapidly spread abroad that China's artistic legacy was being deliberately destroyed – fears that were not allayed by the almost total silence on the part of the Chinese authorities.

It was not until 1971 that rumours began to circulate of sensational archaeological discoveries that had been made during the previous five years. In the spring of 1972 publication of two archaeological journals, *Kaogu* and *Wen Wu*, was resumed, and articles on archaeology began once more to appear in *China Reconstructs* and the *Peking Review*. Now it became clear that archaeology and conservation had in fact never stopped, but had been quietly going on even while the Cultural Revolution was at its height.

If this requires explanation, Chairman Mao has himself given the answer, in his slogan *Ku wei chin yung*, 'make the past serve the present'. It was not old things that were to be repudiated, he said, but old attitudes of mind. Indeed, we have much to learn from the past. 'A splendid old culture', he wrote in 1940, 'was created during the long period of Chinese feudal society. To study the development of this old culture, to reject its feudal dross and assimilate its democratic essence is a necessary condition for developing our new national culture and increasing our national self-confidence.' And again, in 1945: 'Ancient Chinese culture should neither be totally rejected nor blindly copied, but should be accepted discriminatingly so as to help the progress of China's new culture.' How could Chinese ancient culture be studied and 'accepted discriminatingly' unless it were cherished and preserved? There is nothing in the philosophy of the new China that advocates or condones destruction of her artistic heritage.

In fact, there has certainly been less destruction or loss abroad of Chinese works of art during the last twenty-two years than in any comparable period in China's modern history. As we read the dire story of the wholesale burning and looting of palaces, temples and art collections down the centuries it often seems a miracle that anything survived from early times at all; while from the 'opening of China' after the Opium Wars of the nineteenth century until 1949, a steady, ever-increasing flood of Chinese antiquities flowed out of the country into foreign museums and collections. That has now ceased.

Chinese civilization is often thought to be of great antiquity. In fact, it is not as old as that of ancient Egypt or Mesopotamia; but it has been developing continuously since the founding of the first historical dynasty, the Shang, probably between 1600 and 1500 BC. It is worth spending a few moments in contemplating the simplified dynastic chart on page 7, for it shows the great wave-like rhythm of Chinese history as no mere list of dates could do. The major dynasties represent, in their early decades at least, an era of consolidation and settled prosperity after a period of chaos and division which sometimes lasted for several centuries: the Warring States and Ch'in were followed by four hundred years of the Han Dynasty; the Six Dynasties, Ten Kingdoms and Sui by the three centuries of the T'ang; the brief fragmentation of the Five Dynasties by the Sung.

Important developments and innovations in the arts often took place during the unsettled periods, when orthodoxy gave way to independence and freedom from traditional restraints. These new developments then were consolidated into a new orthodoxy when China was united and powerful, giving the art of each major dynasty a distinctive character of its own. That the flavour of the art changed within the dynasty goes without saying: it is a far cry, for example, from the monumental, classical landscape paintings of early Northern Sung to the romanticism of late Southern Sung. But a consistent thread runs through Sung art that was abruptly broken at the fall of the dynasty. So it is natural to think of the development of Chinese art, as the Chinese themselves do, broadly in terms of dynastic styles.

If it were not for the extravagant burial practices of ancient China, we would have only the dimmest picture of Chinese art before the Sung Dynasty. Chinese architecture is chiefly of wood. *All* the palaces and mansions built in the Sung Dynasty and earlier, and nearly all the temple buildings, have been completely destroyed or rebuilt. Apart from fortifications such as the Great Wall, there are in China today no ruins above ground remotely comparable in age and grandeur to those of the Acropolis, the Roman Forum, or even Ravenna. With the buildings there vanished also the great cycles of wall paintings, now known only from literary descriptions of them. Emperors repeatedly creamed off the still surviving masterpieces of painting and took them into the palace, where time and again the imperial collection was destroyed when the dynasty fell. Private collections also were often scattered and destroyed in the times of troubles. Today not a single original work by Wu Tao-tzu, the 'Michelangelo' of T'ang China, survives, and only a handful of scrolls attributed to the masters of the Northern Sung (i.e. before 1125) have come down to us.

Most of the surviving relics of ancient Chinese art come, like those of the Etruscans, from tombs. Confucius said that we understand so little about this life that it is a waste of time to discuss the next. Nevertheless, while vague about its exact nature, the Chinese until recent times always believed that they could take into the next world the things that they had enjoyed, or would like to have enjoyed, in this. So when, partly under pressure from Confucius himself, the immolating of slaves was abandoned in the late Chou Dynasty, the practice arose of substituting replicas of straw, wood, or more often clay. These included not only slaves, but guardians, musicians, jugglers and dancing girls, while the more practical requirements of the departed were met by watchtowers, farmyards, carts and pigsties, and vessels for the storage of food and wine. The number of objects one might put in the tomb was regulated according to the occupant's rank, but the sumptuary laws were often abused. As a result, huge quantities of these models and figurines, called *ming-ch'i*, 'spirit objects', were interred. Only certain objects were made especially for burial. Prominent among them were funerary jades, because jade was supposed to preserve the body from decay. The obsessive belief in the preservative power of jade was dramatically shown by the recent discovery in the tombs at Man-ch'eng near Peking of the corpses of a Western Han prince and princess clad in complete suits of jade, one of which is illustrated.

24–25

Many of the *ming-ch'i* were vessels such as were probably used in the household. Wealthier families buried with the dead not only pottery and porcelain but jewellery, gold and silver vessels, bronze and lacquer, and even on occasion the deceased's favourite paintings. The practice of filling the tomb with *ming-ch'i* declined after the T'ang Dynasty, and was eventually replaced, for all but the wealthiest, by the burning of paper models outside the tomb.

## CHINESE DYNASTIES

| | | | |
|---|---|---|---|
| SHANG | | | c. 1550–c. 1027 BC |
| CHOU | Western Chou<br>Spring & Autumn Period<br>Warring States | c. 1027–771<br>722–481<br>480–221 | 1027–256 |
| CH'IN | | | 221–202 |
| HAN | Former Han<br>Later Han | 202 BC–AD 9<br>AD 25–220 | 202 BC–AD 220 |
| THREE KINGDOMS | | | 220–265 |
| SIX (Chinese) DYNASTIES | Western Chin<br>Eastern Chin<br>Sung<br>Ch'i<br>Liang<br>Ch'en | 265–317<br>317–420<br>420–479<br>479–502<br>502–557<br>557–589 | 265–589 |
| NORTHERN (Foreign) DYNASTIES | Northern Wei<br>Eastern Wei<br>Western Wei<br>Northern Ch'i<br>Northern Chou | 386–535<br>534–543<br>535–554<br>550–577<br>557–581 | 386–581 |
| SUI | | | 581–618 |
| T'ANG | | | 618–906 |
| FIVE DYNASTIES | | | 907–960 |
| NORTHERN SUNG | Liao<br>Chin | 907–1125<br>1115–1234 | 960–1126 |
| SOUTHERN SUNG | | | 1127–1279 |
| YÜAN | | | 1279–1368 |
| MING | | | 1368–1644 |
| CH'ING | | | 1644–1912 |
| REPUBLIC | | | 1912–1949 |
| PEOPLE'S REPUBLIC | | | 1949– |

Tunhuang

MONGOLIA

Wu-wei

KANSU

Ch'i-chia-p'ing

Pan-shan
Mai-chi-shan

SZECHWA

Chengtu

Ta-tsu
CHUNGKING

KWEIC

YÜNNAN

KUNMING
Shih-chai-shan

KV

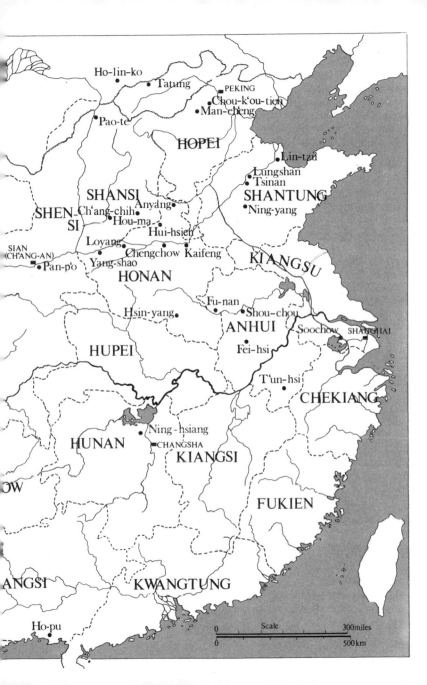

Ho-lin-ko
Tatung
PEKING
Chou-k'ou-tien
Man-chêng
Pao-tê
HOPEI
Lin-tzŭ
Lungshan
Tsinan
SHANSI
Anyang
SHANTUNG
SHEN-
SI
Ch'ang-chih
Ning-yang
Hou-ma
Hui-hsien
Loyang
SIAN
(CH'ANG-AN)
Chengchow Kaifeng
KIANGSU
Pan-p'o
Yang-shao
HONAN
Fu-nan
Hsin-yang
Shou-chou
ANHUI
Soochow
SHANGHAI
HUPEI
Fei-hsi
T'un-hsi
CHEKIANG
Ning-hsiang
HUNAN
CHANGSHA
KIANGSI
OW
FUKIEN
ANGSI
KWANGTUNG
Ho-pu

Scale
0          300miles
0               500km

## Prehistoric China

At the time of writing, the history of man in early China can be traced back about 600,000 years, to a hominid of which a skull was found in 1964 in Lan-t'ien-hsien in Shansi. This Lan-t'ien creature is perhaps a hundred thousand years older than the well-known Peking Man, *Sinanthropus pekinensis*, whose skull was discovered in 1929 in a deep cave at Chou-k'ou-tien southwest of Peking. In late 1941 or 1942 the remains of Peking Man mysteriously disappeared from a warehouse in North China, although the loss has been partly made up by recent finds. Fragments of another fossil skull of Peking Man, and stone implements, were found in 1966 at Chou-k'ou-tien, while excavation of other sites in Shansi and Honan has revealed how widely the Lower Paleolithic Culture was spread across North China.

Gradually in the Late Pleistocene era the evolution of man in China gathered pace. In the 'Upper Cave' at Chou-k'ou-tien have been found remains of *Homo sapiens* (*c.* 20,000 BC), who made tools and ornaments of stone, bone, and shell. Remains of a microlithic culture have been found in Central, South and West China. The Neolithic Revolution began, perhaps 12,000 years ago, when the early Chinese ceased to be hunters and fishermen, settled down, began to build villages and develop the arts of farming and horticulture. The first Neolithic remains with their characteristic painted pottery were found by Gunnar Andersson in 1921 at Yang-shao-ts'un in Honan, and later in Kansu. But the great expansion of Neolithic archaeology dates from after Liberation. By 1972, five thousand Neolithic sites had been discovered, and about two hundred of them excavated. The most spectacular is the cluster of villages discovered in 1953 at Pan-p'o-ts'un, in Shensi, of which a typical area has been roofed over and opened to the public as a museum of Neolithic civilization.

It was long thought that the picture of Neolithic civilization in China was fairly simple: a red and painted pottery culture (Yang-shao) in North and Northwest China, a somewhat later black burnished pottery culture (Lung-shan) in the North and Northeast that in some areas moved in and succeeded it, and grey pottery everywhere. But this picture has been radically altered by the discoveries of recent years. Although there is relatively more painted pottery in the Northwest and North, and more black pottery in the Northeast, the relationship between the two is by no means clear. In some sites the black appears above the red and is therefore later; in others they appear together; while it now seems that the mature black burnished ware of Shantung (Lung-shan) is a late and purely regional development of a culture that stretched across North China.

One of the most important developments since 1950 has been the opening up of South and Southeast China, an area hitherto almost uncharted in Chinese archaeology. Two decades of work in hundreds of sites shows that the Neolithic culture of this area, influenced by both Yang-shao and Lung-shan, persisted long after the coming of bronze technology to the North. The Southeast Neolithic has distinct characteristics of its own, notably a fondness for pottery stamped with repeated geometric designs. This forms a link with Southeast Asia, where the tradition of geometric stamped pottery has continued up to recent centuries. It was also under the influence of this technique that the Southeastern craftsmen decorated bronzes of the Chou period in a style quite unlike that of North China. Two

10, 11

of them are illustrated.

The last main phase of Neolithic culture is represented in North China by a group of sites in and around Ch'i-chia-p'ing in Kansu. In several of these sites simple cast copper ornaments and small tools were found, firm proof that metal technology was not imported fully developed into Shang culture from Western Asia, as has sometimes been suggested, but developed independently from very humble beginnings in China itself.

Until recently the dating of the Chinese Neolithic culture was very much a matter of guesswork. Andersson, for instance, had put his Yang-shao culture about 3500–3000 BC. Writing in 1971, Wu Ju-kang, a leading member of the Chinese Academy of Sciences, estimated the earliest Chinese pottery to be about 10,000 years old. This is very much earlier than any dates that had been suggested before for Chinese Neolithic artifacts, but it is in line with the dating for roughly comparable Japanese pottery of the Jōmon period, which has been firmly established by the Carbon[14] method. In 1972 the first Chinese Carbon[14] dates were published from well-known Neolithic sites in Kansu. Some of these appear, by contrast, to be rather later than was expected. Organic material from the middle Neolithic village of Pan-p'o, for example, has been dated 4115 BC $\pm$ 110 years; from Pan-shan, where Andersson found his most beautiful painted urns, 2065 BC $\pm$ 100 years, from Ch'i-chia-p'ing 1725 and 1695 $\pm$ 95 years. The Carbon[14] method is being used in several research centres, and many more results may be expected. At the time of writing, the thermoluminescence technique for dating pottery had not yet been used in China.

## The Shang Dynasty (c. 1550–1027? BC)

The Shang is the first dynasty in Chinese history of which written records survive, chiefly in the form of inscriptions on 'oracle bones' and on the bronze ritual vessels used in sacrifices to ancestral spirits. Their arts show that the Shang had cultural contacts with the steppe and forest peoples to the north as well as the more primitive tribes to the south. While the ritual bronzes of the later centuries of the Shang have been admired and collected for a thousand years or more, it was only early in the twentieth century that the remains of a Shang city was found at Anyang in Northern Honan. There the first scientific excavations were begun by the Academia Sinica in 1928. The artifacts in pottery, carved marble and bone, and particularly the bronze vessels used in sacrifices to clan ancestors, revealed a high civilization. Clearly these represented not the beginning of a tradition, but its climax. Yet for several decades no earlier Shang remains were found that might account for them.

The vast construction projects on the North China plain since Liberation have now revealed the remains of at least two Shang cities even older than Anyang. In 1954, beneath and around modern Chengchow, traces were found of a city which is almost certainly the middle Shang capital Ao. The site is clearly stratified: the earliest levels being late Neolithic (Lung-shan), followed by Bronze Age (Ao?), followed in turn by a period of decay after the fourteenth century BC when the capital was moved to Anyang. Then in 1958, at Erh-li-t'ou between Chengchow and Loyang, a very early Bronze Age site was discovered, with small metal objects such as spearheads and a bell, and traces of a bronze foundry. This is believed to be Po, site of the capital of the first Shang ruler, known to history as T'ang Wang.

These discoveries have helped to establish a firm chronology for the evolution of the bronze art in the Shang Dynasty, and show how the magical and protective zoomorphic designs developed from the simple motifs on the Chengchow vessels – the bronze objects from Erh-li-t'ou seem not to have been decorated – into the richly integrated décor of the final phase at Anyang.

Discoveries made during and since the Cultural Revolution have added still further to our picture of Shang culture, its extent and its relations with the last phase of the Stone Age in China. In 1966, for example, far to the east of Anyang, a group of typical Shang tombs was found in I-tu-hsien in Shantung Province, containing sacrificial victims, glazed pottery and executioner's axes decorated with masks. In 1971, at Pao-te just inside the Great Wall in North Shansi, a hoard of bronze vessels and other relics of the early Anyang phase was found, the first time that remains of Shang culture have been discovered so far north.

At Anyang itself (Hou-kang) in 1971, a stratified site was discovered showing a continuous sequence of levels from Yang-shao-type pottery and stone tools through to graves of the Shang, Chou and Warring States. In December of the same year a hoard of inscribed ox shoulder-blades was found at Anyang. One of these, in sixty characters, gives instructions about imperial sacrifices and is the longest Shang inscription yet discovered. The beautiful vessel 6 illustrated was unearthed by workers in 1966 and 1970 near Changsha, far to the south of the Shang realm. It is thought that it may have been buried there by Shang nobles fleeing south from the advancing Chou at the fall of the Dynasty.

## The Chou Dynasty (1127 ?–256 BC)

When the Chou invaders moved eastwards and conquered the Shang they adopted many Shang rites and customs, arts and crafts. The first Chou kings, ruling from the region of modern Sian, parcelled out their realm into feudal fiefs. The early Chou was a period of huge territorial expansion, during which Chinese civilization hardly progressed much beyond the level achieved by the Shang at Anyang. But in 771 the Chou moved their capital eastwards to Loyang, and Chinese culture began once more to advance, to blossom paradoxically in the period of incessant warfare between the now powerful and independent territories that marked the last three centuries of the Chou Dynasty, the era often called the Warring States.

The Warring States was a period of important advances in technology, of which the chief was the introduction of iron tools for agriculture, of new economic prosperity based on interstate commerce, and of the rise of wealthy landowners and merchants who spread artistic patronage far beyond the feudal courts, many of which had been swallowed up in the wars that finally ended in 221 BC in the unification of all China by the state of Ch'in. The late Chou was also the period of the great philosophers, Confucius, Mencius and Lao Tzu, of the birth of scholarship and lyric poetry, and of a new level of achievement in the arts and crafts. The oldest silk painting yet discovered belongs to this period, while jade carving, metalwork (including gold and silver inlaying) and fine lacquer and textiles were produced to meet the taste of a new leisured class, and the ever-increasing demand for utensils to bury with the dead.

Before 1950, there had been an enormous amount of random digging and robbing of Chou sites, chiefly of Warring States tombs in the Loyang region; but hardly a single site had been properly investigated, with the exception of those surveyed by Japanese archaeologists during

World War II, such as the Chou State capital at Han-tan. The dating of Chou bronzes was very approximate, while the dating on stylistic grounds of what were thought to be Chou period jades was even more uncertain.

All this dramatically changed immediately after Liberation. In 1950, at Hwi-hsien in Honan, a late Chou burial with nineteen chariots was expertly uncovered. In Shensi, excavation began in 1955 on the sites of the capitals of the first Western Chou rulers to the west of the modern city of Sian. Near Loyang the walls of the gigantic Eastern Chou capital Wang-ch'eng have been traced, with the later Han Dynasty city of Honan nestling comfortably inside it. By 1966, the sites of no less than twenty-one capitals and cities of the Warring States had been found, and the discovery of many dated or dateable tombs has made it possible to establish a clear chronology for bronze and jade, and at the same time shows wide regional differences in artistic styles as each state shaped and decorated its bronzes in its own fashion. Notable finds were a richly furnished tomb of the obscure state of Kuo (about 650 BC) discovered in 1956–57 during the construction of a large dam in the San-men Gorge in Honan; and an important tomb of a Ts'ai state prince, dateable by the inscriptions on the bronzes to 518–491 BC.

Since 1966 a number of superb early Western Chou bronzes have been unearthed, such as the unique creature from Chishan County in Shensi, found in 1970, and the group of late Western Chou vessels found at Ching-shan, Hupeh. The capital of the feudal state of Ch'i has been under excavation at Lin-tzu in Shantung, while important Eastern Chou ritual objects of a kind never seen before were found at Hou-ma in Shansi. The classical text Li-chi, Record of Rites, described the institution of oath-swearing in feudal China, how horses, cows, pigs and chickens, according to the swearer's rank, were sacrificed, how the oath was written on a tablet, the text smeared with the animal's blood, read out and then buried with the offering in a pit. At Hou-ma an oath-swearing site of the State of Chou was discovered in 1969–70, with over four hundred such pits, containing the remains of sacrificial animals, inscribed oath-swearing tablets (meng-shu) and jade and other votive objects exactly as the Li-chi had described them. This discovery suggests that the Li-chi, and its companion the Chou-li (Rites of Chou), which were lost at the fall of Chou and rewritten from memory in the Han Dynasty, may be more reliable guides to Chou customs than was generally thought. This fact is important for the study of Chinese art, as these texts describe the organization of arts and crafts under the Chou in some detail.

Confucius, like Pythagoras, upheld music as an aid to good government and the creation of a harmonious society. Prominent among the instruments used in ancient ritual music were sets of bronze bells and stone chimes of graded sizes suspended from a wooden frame and struck with a wooden hammer. Many sets of bells have been discovered, and some of plain stone chimes, but none comparable to the set of twenty-five chimes exquisitely painted with phoenixes and other motifs which were unearthed in 1971 at Chiang-ling in Hupeh. Unfortunately the colour is too delicate to survive reproduction in a book of this size.

Chiang-ling lay within the territory of the State of Ch'u, which occupied a huge era of central China, and in 223 BC was almost the last great state to succumb to the all-devouring power of Ch'in. Ch'u was the home of China's first nature philosophers and rhapsodic poets, and of styles in art, notably in inlaid bronze and carved and lacquered wood-work, even more elegant and fanciful than the decorative arts of North China. Square stamped sheets of gold money found in 1969 and 1970 at Liu-an and Fu-nan in Anhui testify to the prosperity of Ch'u in the late Chou period. The oldest known Chinese painting on silk (third century BC) was found at Changsha before World War II, and in recent years many waterlogged timber tombs have been found in and near the city, their contents miraculously preserved by a 'filter' of white clay and charcoal that surrounded the
17–22 elaborate system of inner and outer coffins. An important Ch'u tomb found in 1956 at Hsin yang, in southern Honan, contained not only carved and lacquered wooden furniture and shields, but a 25-stringed zither (*se*) and one of the extraordinary antlered and long-tongued cult objects thought to have been worshipped in fertility or rain-bringing rites,
13 or used as a guardian of the dead. In 1971 a richly furnished and relatively early Ch'u tomb was discovered at Liu-ch'eng-ch'iao, Changsha, containing a 23-stringed zither, rolls of silk cloth and bronze axes with their wood and rattan hafts still intact. An even more remarkable discovery was the Han tomb at Ma-wang-tui, described below.

## The Ch'in Dynasty (221–202 BC) and the Han Dynasty (202 BC–AD 220)

In 221 BC the Ch'in king conquered Ch'i and finally achieved the unification of all the former feudal states under his rule, naming himself Shih-huang-ti, the First Emperor. While he suppressed all literature and scholarship which might have cast doubt upon the legitimacy of his dynasty, he established by extremely harsh methods a degree of political, economic and cultural unity over the conquered states that laid the foundations for the structure of China as we know it. His son was incompetent and lost the mandate to the Han Dynasty, which consolidated his achievement on humaner lines, vastly enlarged China's boundaries, established colonies in Korea and Indochina, and reached out into Central Asia, opening the way to commerce and cultural traffic with the Near East and India. The Former or Western Han (202 BC–AD 9) had its capital at Hsien-yang in Shensi, followed after a short interregnum by the Later or Eastern Han (AD 25–220), with its capital at Honan, the walled city to the east of modern Loyang which we have already mentioned.

The arts of the Han Dynasty reflect the boundless vigour of the new nation and the variety of local cultures and traditions that flourished in different parts of the empire. This was a time when the folklore and superstitions of many areas were eagerly accepted at the capital; when almost everyone, from the emperor down, believed in magic, in elixirs of immortality and in the spirits that dwelt in mountains and rivers; while the opening of the Silk Road to the west not only brought foreign products and artistic styles to China and Chinese silks to Syria and the markets of Rome, but also stirred the imagination with dreams of fabulous lands and people beyond the deserts that were China's natural frontiers. All these themes appear in Han art, giving it a special vigour and variety.

Never was so much labour and wealth spent on the dead as in the Han Dynasty. The tombs of the Ch'in and Han emperors seem all to have been plundered centuries ago and right up to 1949 the plundering went on. Now, of course, all this has changed. Among great numbers of Han tombs that have been excavated and recorded since then we need only mention a few by way of example: in the far northeast at I-nan in Shantung, the large stone-chambered tomb decorated with lively and extremely detailed engraved pictures, of the third century AD; at the opposite corner of China, the early Han graves at Shih-chai-shan in Yünnan,

*32* with bronze drum-shaped containers for cowrie-shells crowded with ritual, war and hunting scenes modelled in the round; important tombs decorated with wall-paintings at Wang-tu in Hopei (discovered in 1952), at Ts'ao-yüants'un in Shansi (1959), and at Liang-shan in Shantung (1953); while wooden grave figurines, hitherto found only in Ch'u graves in the Changsha region, have now been discovered at Chengtu in Szechwan, and at Wu-wei far to the northwest in the dry sands of Kansu.

These finds have at least been equalled by those made since 1966. By far the most spectacular were the tombs of the Han prince Liu Sheng (died 113 BC), elder brother of the great Emperor Wu, and of his wife Tou Wan, which were accidentally discovered in 1968 by members of the People's Liberation Army at Man-ch'eng, about 140 kilometers southwest of Peking. Both are shaft tombs cut deep into a rocky hillside. The entrance passage, with side shafts crammed with vessels and carriages, opens out into a large chamber containing the remains of a wooden, tile-roofed structure which has collapsed, beyond which lies the coffin chamber itself. Liu Sheng also had a private 'bathroom'.

In both the main and inner chambers a great variety of
*24–29* *ming-ch'i* in jade, bronze, gilt bronze and lacquer were set out, with pottery and stone figurines, totalling over 2,800 objects. Many are in perfect condition still, for secure behind their entrance walls of cast iron these tombs, like that of Tutankhamun, had never been disturbed. Some of the objects are familiar Han types though of unmatched
*29* quality: the inlaid bronze hill-censer, for example, is even more beautiful and more delicately made than the celebrated censer in the Freer Gallery, Washington. But many others are unique, among them the figure of a kneeling

26  palace girl in gilt bronze holding a lamp inscribed with the words *ch'ang hsin,* 'eternal fidelity' – the most moving of the treasures yet published from the tomb of Tou Wan.

Although twice robbed in ancient times, a large Han tomb at Lei-t'ai near Wu-wei in Kansu, investigated in 1969, still yielded – not jewels, but treasures of another sort. The 220 pieces of lacquer, bronze, goldsmith's work and other *ming-ch'i* left behind by the robbers include some of the finest Han sculpture yet discovered, notably the galloping horse poised with one hoof resting lightly on a flying

34–35  swallow. This spendid creature is not only a triumph of the Han sculptor's art but a vivid reminder of the almost magic potency that, in the eyes of the Han Chinese, the horse was believed to possess.

Also unique are the pottery objects found in the same year in a Western Han tomb at Tsinan in Shantung. The tray

30–31  with painted figures tumbling and juggling to music before two rows of dignified spectators represents in lively tableau form the kind of entertainments that were often depicted on the walls of the tombs themselves.

Among the many tombs excavated in and around Changsha, the tomb at Ma-wang-tui discovered early in 1972 is the most important, for not only are its contents abundant and so perfectly preserved that the very peaches and pears set out for the dead woman can easily be identi-

18–19, 20–21  fied, but stretched over the corpse was a silk painting in the form of a hanging banner of a type long thought of as having been introduced with Buddhist art from Central Asia after the Han Dynasty. This remarkable scroll is about a thousand years older than any comparable silk scroll painting yet discovered in China, and leaves no doubt that the hanging scroll format is of Chinese origin.

## Three Kingdoms and Six Dynasties (220–581)

When the Han Dynasty collapsed, China broke up into the Three Kingdoms of Wei in the North, Shu-han in the West, and Wu in the Southeast, centred on Nanking. The tormented country was briefly reunited under the Chin Dynasty (263–317) but the nomadic hordes roaming China's northern frontiers took advantage of her weakness, broke through the Great Wall, sacked Loyang and Ch'ang-an, and by 317 had made themselves masters of North China. Eventually a Toba Turkic house calling themselves Northern Wei established a dynasty which, with its barbarian successors, ruled North China for nearly two hundred years.

Under the Turkic rule the North was thoroughly cosmopolitan. Trade and cultural traffic flowed into China from Central Asia, and Buddhism was established as the state religion. The Toba Turks saw the superior merits of Chinese culture, however, recruited the Chinese intelligentsia into their service, and became rapidly sinicized. It was chiefly under their patronage that the great series of Buddhist cave shrines at Yünkang, Lungmen and Tunhuang were carved out and adorned with sculpture and paintings. Today these cave shrines are the chief artistic monuments surviving from the centuries between the Han and the T'ang, and give a quite false impression that the great centres of Chinese art were in the north.

In fact it was Nanking, the capital of 'free China', that was the true hub of Chinese culture during these troubled years. The southern dynasts were corrupt or incompetent or both, but the arts flourished there in a kinder environment than that of North China, and the late fourth, fifth and sixth centuries saw in what is now Chekiang and Kiangsu a renaissance of poetry, the birth of literary criticism and aesthetics, the activity of great calligraphers and figure painters such as Wang Hsi-chih (321–79) and Ku K'ai-chih (c. 340–406), and the beginning of landscape painting as a fine art.

Little of this period except for the cave-shrines and monumental funerary sculpture remains above ground, and most tombs, compared with those of the Han, were poorly furnished. Exceptional is the tomb of a high Chinese official in the service of the Toba Turks named Ssu-ma Chin-lung, who was buried at the Northern Wei capital in 484. Opened in 1965–66, the tomb contained richly carved stone stands and inkstones, fine celadon ware, and gilt-bronze wine-cups of remarkably Sassanian appearance; and, most important of all, several wooden screen panels painted in lacquer with figure subjects, including the ever-popular Virtuous Women of Antiquity. The latter included the upright Lady Pan, who refused to go out with her sovereign in his palanquin lest she distract his thoughts from affairs of state. About eighty years earlier the same story had been illustrated in almost exactly the same fashion by Ku K'ai-chih – if indeed the famous Admonitions scroll in the British Museum is his work, or a copy of it. Whether Ku K'ai-chih invented this treatment, or both derive from a traditional rendering of the theme, is not known.

37

The sculpture of Yünkang and Lungmen, and the wall-paintings of Tunhuang, have long been known, but much conservation and research has been done at these sites since Liberation, while the remote and spectacular cave-shrines at Ping-ling-ssu and Mai-chi-shan in Kansu were surveyed for the first time in the 1950s. Not all the important Buddhist sculpture found since 1949 was in caves, however. In 1943 farmers digging near Ch'ü-yang in Hopei unearthed the first of what turned out to be a hoard of over 2,600 Buddhist figures in stone, thought to have been hastily buried there at the time of the An Lu-shan rebellion in 756. Later excavations proved, from dated pieces, that the important Ch'ü-yang workshops had been active as early as 520. Whether the cause was this same disaster, or the persecution of Buddhism in 845 is not known, but another buried hoard of Buddhist sculpture of the Six Dynasties and T'ang was unearthed at Chengtu in Szechwan; a third was found at Ch'iung-lai not far away. These discoveries are particularly important because so much Buddhist sculpture had been lost to foreign museums before Liberation.

Fig. 1

Fig. 2

*Fig. 1 Standing figure of Śākyamuni; sandstone. Ht. about 2 m. Cave 135, Mai-chi-shan, Kansu Province. Northern Wei Dynasty (c. 520–35).*

Since 1966 the first extensive excavations have been carried out at Tunhuang in the flat fround in front of the caves. The finds published so far include silk textiles *40–41* dated between 477 and 695. So many early Chinese textiles, indeed, have been recovered in recent years in the Northwest and Central Asia that a lavish publication, *The Silk Road*, published in 1972, was devoted to a small selection of more recent finds. Most were the result of many seasons' digging in sites that had been explored after the turn of the century by Sir Aurel Stein, Sven Hedin, Grünwedel and von le Coq. In 1959 excavations were begun at the site of the ruined city of Niya, abandoned in the third century AD, and in the cemeteries at Karakhojo and Astana near Turfan. They have yielded a great variety of stuffs, including silk tapestry, embroidery, damask, batik and tie-and-dye, dating from the Han to the T'ang, many of the later pieces showing *51* Sassanian influence.

To anticipate a little, one of the Chinese contributions to the culture of the Central Asian Kingdoms was dramatically illustrated by the discovery in the campaign of 1966–69 at Turfan of the earliest known, almost complete, manuscript of the *Analects* of Confucius, with the Cheng Hsüan Commentary, dated equivalent to 710 AD. In 1969 a copy of 'The Old Charcoal Seller' by the T'ang poet Po Chü-i (772– 846) was unearthed at Jo-chiang in Sinkiang. It had been carefully written out in the year 820 by a Uighur named Kanmaur, when Po Chü-i was still at the height of his career two thousand miles away – a remarkable instance of the speed with which a popular poet's work in those days of difficult travel reached even beyond the confines of the empire; for by this time the Turfan oasis was under the control of China's Uighur allies.

*Fig. 2 Seated Buddha; red sandstone. Ht. 32.9 cm. From Ch'iung-lai, Szechwan Province. T'ang Dynasty.*

## The Sui Dynasty (581–618) and the T'ang Dynasty (618–906)

Although the first Sui Emperor succeeded in reuniting China, the oppressive and extravagant rule of his son brought his dynasty to an abrupt end. From its ruins rose the T'ang, which for nearly a century and a half grew in extent, power and prosperity, once again establishing China as the dominant cultural force in east Asia. Under the Emperor Hsüan Tsung (Ming Huang, 712–56) the empire was at its height, great poets and painters served at court and the streets of Ch'ang-an (modern Sian) were thronged with foreigners attracted by trade and by the liberal, cosmopolitan atmosphere of the city. The rebellion, in 755–56, of General An Lu-shan, favourite of the Emperor's concubine Yang Kuei-fei, nearly destroyed the dynasty. It recovered, only to sink into a long slow decline that is clearly reflected in the arts and crafts of the second half of the T'ang.

Replanning and construction in Sian since 1949 have uncovered sections of the T'ang capital, and excavation of the site of Ming Huang's palace, the Ta Ming Kung, beyond the northern walls, was begun in 1957. All that remains of the palace today are the marble terraces and the foundations of halls of state, in the ruins of which a few splendid silver dishes were found. The vast majority of T'ang tombs also have been plundered of all but their worthless ceramic vessels and figurines. These have happily survived in great quantities, to show how boldly T'ang potters experimented with coloured glazes, how confidently they borrowed forms and motifs from Western Asia, and with what lively humour they depicted the foreign traders and entertainers who were attracted by the prosperity of Ch'ang-an and Loyang.

Until very recently our picture of T'ang decorative arts was based largely upon chance finds from the few tombs that had not been plundered, and upon the treasures placed in 756 in the Shōsōin Repository at Nara in Japan, most of which are Chinese, or made in the Chinese style. In 1970, however, two large earthenware jars were discovered in the southern suburbs of Sian, containing over two thousand separate objects which included fine examples of gold-smiths' and silversmiths' work that rival some of the pieces in the Shōsōin. There were medical instruments, boxes containing precious minerals, and Sassanian, Byzantine and Japanese coins. The hoard was buried at the site of the mansion of a cousin of the Emperor Ming Huang, Prince Pin, who died in 741. It is thought that these precious objects were hastily, if carefully, buried by his son at the time of An Lu-shan's advance on Ch'ang-an in 756, and that the owner then quit Ch'ang-an – perhaps in the entourage of Ming Huang on his precipitate flight to Szechwan – and never returned to recover his treasures.

While a good deal is known about Sui and T'ang Buddhist pictorial arts from the banners and wall-painting, the work of the great masters of figure painting is almost all lost. Since 1950, however, important tombs of the seventh and eighth centuries in the Sian region have been discovered, among them those of imperial princes and princesses. The tomb chamber and 'spirit way' (entrance passage) are decorated with figures of officials, guards, attendants and servants doing honour to the dead, and in one case with horsemen in landscapes. They vary a good deal in quality, for they were not to be seen again by mortal eyes, and the paintings are mostly rather sketchily done. The most beautiful are the wall-paintings in the tomb, discovered in 1962, of the princess Yung-t'ai, seventh daughter of the Emperor Chung Tsung and granddaughter of the monstrous empress Wu who in 701 murdered her, or perhaps allowed her to commit suicide, at the age of seventeen, with her husband and brothers. When her father regained his throne in 705 he had Yung-t'ai sumptuously reinterred in a deep underground tomb in Ch'ien-hsien, west of Sian. The walls of the passageway are decorated with paintings of male servants and warriors, while the twin inner chambers bear the charming and elegant figures of serving girls. These are the finest secular wall-paintings of this period yet discovered, and were very probably executed by a major court artist, perhaps a pupil of the great Yen Li-pen who had died in 673. The paintings were removed for preservation, and today the visitor will find copies in their place.

## Sung Dynasty (960–1279)

After another period of division (the Five Dynasties, 907–60), China was reunited under the Sung. But the new dynasty was very different from the confident, extrovert, expansionist T'ang. Now China faced a constant threat from the barbarians on her northern frontiers who were bought off with ever-increasing amounts of 'Danegeld' paid in money and luxury goods. In 1127 the northern capital Pien-ching (modern Kaifeng) fell to the Jurchen Tartars, who set up their own dynasty over North China, the Chin. The remnants of the court fled to Hangchow, where the Sung sank into a long twilight, and finally into the darkness of the Mongol occupation of the whole of China in 1279.

Sung culture was inward-looking, devoted to scholarship, philosophy, arts and letters. The emperors, as a whole, were more enlightened and humane than any before or since, and there was, for the first half of the dynasty at least, an accord between the scholars and the court that stimulated the arts. Painting in this period reached a climax of monumental realism. By contrast, artists of the Southern Sung gave way to an exquisite romanticism, or took refuge in a purely private search for truth through Zen expressionism. The crafts of the Sung Dynasty, notably porcelain, reflect the cultivation of their courtly and scholarly patrons.

Owing to the destruction of the imperial collection in 1127, very few Northern Sung paintings have survived. In recent years a small number of important works have come to light in China, some previously in private hands, and these have gone a little way towards building up the national collections which had suffered so severely when most of the contents of the Peking and Nanking museums were taken to Taiwan in 1948. Most remarkable among these post-1949 discoveries is the *Ch'ing-ming shang-ho t'u* ('Going up River at the Spring Festival Picture'), a panoramic landscape depicting the suburbs of the Northern Sung

Fig. 3 The heretical teachers slander the Buddha: stone sculpture in high relief. Ht. approximately 130 cm. At Ta-tsu, Szechwan Province. Sung Dynasty.

*Fig. 4 Head of the monk Mahākāśyapa, disciple of the Buddha. Clay plaster. Cave 90, Mai-chi-shan, Kansu Province. Sung Dynasty.*

capital early in the twelfth century. Many later and somewhat fanciful copies of the scroll are known, but the original, now in Peking, is a monument to the climax in pictorial realism that was achieved at the end of Northern Sung, only to be abandoned again until modern times.

Significant discoveries have also been made in the realm of ceramics, which reached in the Sung Dynasty a perfect balance between the natural vigour of the earlier T'ang wares and the perfect finish of those of Ming and Ch'ing. While the mysterious Ch'ai ware, with a glaze 'blue as the sky after rain', remains as elusive as ever, many Sung kilns have now been located, and it is now possible, for example, to determine which of the many varieties of 'Tz'u-chou ware' (North China decorated stoneware) came from which kilns, while it has been established that several quite

57

*Fig. 5 Condemned souls in the Hell of Cold and Ice. Stone sculpture. Height about 75 cm. At Ta-tsu, Szechwan Province. Sung Dynasty.*

different types of ware were often made in the same factory. The extension of scientific archaeology into South China has located some of the kilns which produced wares for export to Southeast Asia, Indonesia and the Philippines.

A new chapter in the study of Chinese sculpture in the Sung Dynasty opened with the discovery of the Mai-chi-shan caves already referred to and the publication of a little-known sculptured cliff at Ta-tsu in Szechwan, dating chiefly from the Sung. The lively realism of the Ta-tsu high relief figures, some of which resemble the clay figures at Mai-chi-shan, others reminiscent of mediaeval European sculpture, is further proof that beside the courtly and scholarly arts for which the Sung is famous there flourished a vigorous school of popular Buddhist art of a very different character.

*Fig. 1*

*Figs. 3, 5*
*Fig. 4*

## The Yüan Dynasty (1279–1368) and Later

The Mongol occupation of the whole of the country was a disaster from which Chinese cultural life took decades to recover, and in the process China rejected much that had survived, in dead or dying forms, from the last years of the Sung Dynasty. The scholar painters repudiated the artificiality of the Southern Sung academy style and developed an entirely new school of literary landscape and bamboo painting; while the taste of the Mongol court demanded more elaborate objects such as carved rather than plain lacquer, and in place of the sober delicacy of Sung ceramics, ornate celadons and white porcelain richly decorated with copper red or cobalt blue under the glaze, and such gaudy ware as the polychrome incense burner illustrated on plate 63. The new styles in arts and crafts tried out in the brief and turbulent, but artistically important, Yüan Dynasty were to be consolidated by the Ming and further refined by the Ch'ing.

In Peking itself, the large-scale replanning of the city and removal of the walls have led to the discovery of the remains of Ta-tu, the original Mongol capital of Kublai Khan, founded in 1267. The ramparts, gates and some streets of this city have been traced and the foundations of several noblemen's mansions have been revealed. Beneath one lay a cache of sixteen pieces of porcelain, including some of the earliest blue and white yet scientifically excavated. In another was found a fragment of a lacquer plate inlaid with mother-of-pearl – again one of the few Yüan pieces in this technique that can be securely dated.

It is rare to find a richly furnished tomb entirely undisturbed, and the discovery in 1970 in Tsou-hsien, Shantung, of the tomb of Chu Tan, tenth son of the first Ming Emperor Hung Wu (1368–98) is of particular importance. Chu Tan, Prince of Lu, who died in 1389 at the

59

58

*Fig. 6 Figurines from the tomb of Chu Tan; painted wood. Average ht. about 29 cm. From Tsou-hsien, Shantung Province. Ming Dynasty.*

*Fig. 6*
age of nineteen, was buried with about a thousand objects, among them over four hundred carved wooden figurines, a Sung Dynasty zither, jade vessels, and the prince's personal wardrobe. The prince also took with him to the grave three hundred volumes of Yüan printed books, a fan painting inscribed in gold by the Sung Emperor Kao Tsung, scrolls of calligraphy, and a scroll painting of lotus flowers bearing the signature and inscription of the great early Yüan painter Ch'ien Hsüan (c. 1235–after 1300). Even more sumptuous, and already well-known, are the contents of the tomb of the late Ming Emperor Wan-li (1573–1620), discovered in 1956, and since put on view to the public in Peking.

The opening of these great tombs – and more excavations of Ming and Ch'ing imperial and princely tombs may be expected – not only saves what remains underground from inevitable eventual destruction, but fulfils China's pledge to give back to the people what they themselves have created. While this work continues, we in the West can only admire the scrupulous care with which it is carried out, benefit from the immense increase in the amount of material available for study, and rejoice that these treasures are now being brought out of the darkness and into the light of day.

## Notes on the Figures

*Fig. 1*    Standing figure of Śākyamuni; sandstone. Ht. about 2 m.
Cave 135. Mai-chi-shan, Kansu. Northern Wei Dynasty
(*c*. 520–35).
This is the central figure of a triad standing in the middle of
the cave chamber, high up on the southwest face of the cliff.
The 184 cave-shrines and sculpture groups of Mai-chi-shan
were first surveyed by a Chinese archaeological team in
1952–53. While Tunhuang is famous for its wall-paintings,
what remains at Mai-chi-shan is chiefly its sculpture in clay
plaster. This is one of the few stone figures in the caves, and
a superb example of the mature second phase of Buddhist
sculpture when Indian and Central Asian styles were
flattened, made linear rather than plastic – in other words,
completely sinicized. This figure is so close in style to the
principal Buddha groups in the Pin-yang cave at Lungmen,
an imperial dedication probably completed in 523, that it is
not inconceivable that it was carved by workmen from the
same *atelier*. The pink sandstone is not native to the mountain, however, and where this masterpiece was carved, and
how it was hauled up the face of the cliff and through the
narrow chamber entrance 150 feet from the ground, remain
a mystery.

*Fig. 2*    Seated Buddha; red sandstone. Ht. 32.9 cm. From Ch'iung-
lai, Szechwan Province. T'ang Dynasty.
This is one of over two hundred pieces of Buddhist sculpture
discovered in 1947 when a flood of the Ts'u River carried
away part of the river bank near the Ta-fu Temple outside
the West Gate of Ch'iung-lai city. A selection of the most
interesting pieces was published in 1959. It is not known
for certain how the sculpture came to be buried, but
Chinese authorities suggest that it occurred at the time of

the proscription of Buddhism and the destruction of most Buddhist temples in 845.

Most of the pieces are fairly small, the amplitude of their modelling and richness of sculptural treatment giving them a rather deceptive impression of heroic size. The T'ang Buddhist sculpture of Szechwan lacks the refinement of the best of the North China work – at Ch'ü-yang in Hopei, for instance, where another T'ang hoard has been found. But it is confident and vigorous. The treatment of this figure is echoed in sculpture at Mai-chi-shan (for example, in the seated Maitreya of Cave 43) which was partly under the influence of the Szechwan school.

*Fig. 3*    The heretical teachers slander the Buddha: stone sculpture in high relief. Ht. approximately 130 cm. From Ta-tsu, Szechwan Province. Sung Dynasty.

The remarkable sculpture on the cliff face and in niches at Ta-tsu, west of Chungking, has become widely known in China only since the publication of a monograph in Peking in 1959, and it is still today almost unknown abroad. The principal carvings are ranged round a narrow V-shaped valley, about 1,600 feet long and 160 feet high, and there are a dozen smaller sites in the neighbourhood. Most of the work at Ta-tsu itself was commissioned by a famous twelfth-century Buddhist monk, Chao Chih-feng (1159–after 1220) who spent his lifetime in raising funds and commissioning craftsmen.

While some of the Ta-tsu groups depict orthodox Buddhist doctrine, others illustrate the popular religion which was a lively mixture of Buddhist, Taoist and Confucian teachings. The main Buddha groups are rather heavy and conventional in style, but the scenes illustrating events in the life of the Buddha, and even more the sins of men and women here on earth and their punishment in the nether regions, are carved with considerable freedom, power and humour and give the viewer the impression that he is watching, frozen forever in stone, the morality plays that were performed in temple courtyards.

The incident depicted here occurred some years after the Enlightenment, when the Buddha's jealous rival Devadatta, with teachers from six heretical sects, embarked upon a campaign against him that did not stop short of attempted murder. The sharp, almost grotesque, modelling of the slanderers' faces reminds us of the heads carved on the corbels and bosses of European cathedrals at about the same time. They also remind us that beside the courtly and scholarly arts for which the Sung Dynasty is famous there existed a vital popular tradition that is little known, and is yet to receive the attention it deserves.

*Fig. 4*   Head of the monk Mahākāśyapa, disciple of the Buddha. Clay plaster. Cave 90, Mai-chi-shan, Kansu Province. Sung Dynasty.
Although this cave was hollowed out and decorated in the Northern Wei Dynasty, the main figures were remodelled in the Sung. This is a fine example of the freedom and vigour of a local school of craftsmanship remote from the chief centres of artistic activity in North China. I wrote of this piece in 1969: 'The head is powerfully conceived, a sense of intense spiritual force being achieved not only in sculptural terms but also by a vigorous linear movement of the modeller's knife. The swiftly cut lines that define the eyebrow, arch over the nostril and round the curving lips are executed with the same sweeping movement of the hand that we find in the brush line of the Chinese painter, proclaiming once again the unity in feeling and expression that exists between painting and sculpture in China.' This head also suggests the exaggeration of the facial features with which the tenth-century Zen painter Kuan-hsiu is said to have endowed his figures; and it may more safely be compared in the intensity of its expression with the well-known set of glazed pottery Lohan of the Liao Dynasty (tenth–eleventh centuries) from I-chou in Hopei Province, one of which is in the British Museum, five in North American collections.

*Fig. 5*   Condemned souls in the Hell of Cold and Ice. Stone sculpture: Height about 75 cm. At Ta-tsu, Szechwan Province. Sung Dynasty.
There were several systems of hells in Chinese popular religion, and without knowing which text is being followed by the carvers here it is impossible to tell what sins these gargoyle-like unfortunates are expiating.

*Fig. 6*   Figurines from the tomb of Chu Tan; painted wood. Average ht. about 29 cm. From Tsou-hsien, Shantung Province. Ming Dynasty.

These figurines are part of a set of 432 humans and horses, with two canopied carriages, placed in the front chamber of the tomb. They include soldiers and guards, servants and attendants, courtiers and entertainers. Some carry weapons, others canopies, fans or musical instruments. One has a stool across his shoulders.

The custom of placing figurines, generally of pottery, in the tomb reached its height in the T'ang Dynasty and then declined. By the Ming it was largely replaced by the burning of paper or straw effigies and models outside the tombs. Ming pottery tomb figurines are uncommon, wooden ones still rarer. This is by far the largest collection ever discovered intact and gives us a fascinating glimpse of Ming ceremonial costume.

## Notes on the Plates

1   Bowl: red pottery painted in black slip. Diam. 38 cm.
    Excavated at Pan-p'o-ts'un, near Sian, Shensi Province.
    Middle Neolithic period, about fourth millennium BC.
    This vessel is decorated with masks, projecting spiked
    triangles, and reticulated rectangles which might possibly
    represent fishing nets. The decoration of Chinese Neolithic
    pottery nearly always consists of abstract and geometric
    motifs whose meaning is not understood. Only a few pieces,
    nearly all from Pan-p'o, bear recognizable pictures of
    objects, chiefly masks, fishes and deer, and what in one case
    may be an elephant. They are the oldest known pictures in
    the history of Chinese art.

2   Water-pitcher in the form of a dog; red pottery. Excavated
    in 1959 at Ta-wen-k'ou, Ning-yang-hsien, Shantung
    Province. Neolithic period.
    This pitcher, which bears a striking and quite fortuitous
    resemblance to certain ancient Peruvian pottery, was exca-
    vated in a Neolithic graveyard which contained chiefly red
    pottery, with a small proportion of painted ware and of the
    black burnished ware formerly thought peculiar to
    Shantung.
    Several sites of the Ta-wen-k'ou type have now been
    discovered, in some of which the red pottery is beneath and
    therefore older than the black. This has led Chinese archae-
    ologists to conclude that the earlier Neolithic civilization of
    Shantung was not the classic Lung-shan, but a mixed
    culture, which Chang Kwang-chih has called 'Lungshanoid',
    from which the Lung-shan is a regional development.

3   Water-pitcher, *kuei*; red pottery. Excavated at Wei-fang,
    Shantung Province. *c*. 2000–1500 BC.

These finely-potted pitchers belong to a late phase of the Lung-shan culture of Shantung. Similar vessels, with hollow legs in the shape of the *li*-tripod later adapted to bronze, were found at Liang-ch'en-chen in Shantung, and at Kao-huang-miao near Hsü-chou in Kiangsu Province, showing the extension of the Lung-shan culture into Southeast China.

4   Ritual food vessel, *chia*; bronze. Ht. 37.3 cm. From Hsiao-nan-chang village, Wen-hsien, Honan Province, about 70 km. northeast of Loyang. Late Shang Dynasty, about twelfth century BC.
This vessel, with twenty-two other Shang bronzes, was discovered in 1968 by peasants levelling ground for planting. The principal decoration, divided into three panels by compact flanges, consists of owls with wings outstretched. The legs and the caps of the posts for lifting the vessel off the fire are decorated with cicadas. Inside the vessel is the single character *hsi*. The meaning of the owl motif is not clear; perhaps it was connected with a particular clan. Some Shang vessels are in the form of owls, and the bird appears on others, but the way they are represented here seems to be unique.

5   Water or wine vessel, *tsun*; stoneware decorated round the shoulder with an impressed geometric pattern and covered with a thin felspathic glaze. Excavated at Chengchow, Honan Province. Shang Dynasty.
The Chinese description calls this 'the earliest porcelain so far discovered in China', but as it is neither vitreous nor translucent we would prefer to call it a high-fired stoneware (the Chinese term *tz'u* may be used for both). Although not a true porcelain, this vessel shows that the Chinese had developed, before the end of the second millennium BC, a degree of sophistication in ceramic technology that was not attained in Europe until the beginning of the eighteenth century.

6   Ritual wine vessel, *yu*; bronze. Ht. 39 cm. Discovered in Ning-hsiang, Hunan Province, in 1970. Late Shang Dynasty, eleventh century BC.

This vessel, inscribed with the single character *ko*, was found by two workers of the Huangtsai People's Commune, 50 km. west-north-west of Changsha. Although of exceptional quality and in fine condition, this *yu* is not unique. A group of very similar vessels, all characterized by bird ornament, a band of horizontal ribbing round the body, strong flanges, and openwork hooks protruding from the lid, is to be found in Western museums, all dating from the last century of the Shang Dynasty. Two things make this vessel of unusual interest: its location and its contents. Ning-hsiang lies far to the south of the Shang realm, and Chinese authorities have suggested that this vessel, and another formed of two owls back-to-back found at Changsha, might have been carried there and buried by Shang nobles fleeing from the advancing Chou at the fall of the dynasty. The vessel when opened was found to contain no less than 329 small, exquisitely fashioned jade objects, including *ch'uan* rings, *chüeh* incomplete rings, *kuan* tubes and pendants, all, like the vessel itself, in a perfect state of preservation.

7   Ritual wine vessel, *tsun*; bronze. The main decoration consists of *t'ao-t'ieh* masks; round the shoulder are *k'uei* dragons, and three openwork flanges alternating with bovine masks in relief. Ht. 47 cm. Found in 1957 in the Fu-nan district of northwestern Anhui Province near the border of Honan. Late Shang or very early Western Chou Dynasty, eleventh–tenth century BC.
This is one of eight bronze vessels found by fishermen in the bed of a canal of the Yüeh-erh River. It has been suggested that they may have been washed into the river from an ancient tomb nearby. No tomb has yet been discovered, however, and they may have formed part of a buried cache. The bold relief and crisp modelling, and the remarkable condition of this vessel, make it a masterpiece of early bronze casting.

8   Ritual food vessel, *ting*; bronze. Ht. 17.8 cm. One of a group of vessels unearthed in 1971 at Hsiao-pa-li-ts'un, near Fei-hsi in Anhui Province. Late Western Chou period, about eighth century BC.

Among the vessels from the Fei-hsi group are several unique pieces. This *ting* is unusual in having hollow legs straight inside and curved with flanges outside; the flat cover was not previously known on three-legged *ting* of the Shang or Western Chou, but is found on *ting* among the later Ts'ai State bronzes and on bronzes from Ch'u State in Central China. This is another example of the extension of the influence of Chou art in a southeasterly direction.

**9**    Ritual wine vessel, *hu*; bronze. Ht. 66 cm. Excavated in 1966 at Ching-shan in Hupei Province. Late Western Chou period, about eighth century BC.
This is one of ninety-seven bronzes discovered at this site, ten of which carry inscriptions. The twelve-character inscription on this vessel says that it was cast by a personage of the State of Tseng. It is a fine example of the elaborate style of the early Spring and Autumn period.

**10**   Ritual wine vessel, *tsun*; bronze. Ht. 26.5 cm. Excavated at An-ch'eng, Wu-ching-hsien, Kiangsu Province. Late Spring and Autumn Period, sixth–fifth century BC.
This piece, recovered in remarkably good condition, was part of a cache of bronzes recovered in 1957 from a moat of the ancient city of Yen in the State of Yüeh. Most of the bronzes from this site are in typical Huai River style, but the decoration of this *tsun* is quite unlike that of North China bronzes of this or indeed any period, being influenced by the technique of stamping and impressing close-knit designs in pottery that was practised in this southeastern part of China from the Neolithic period down to the Han Dynasty. The fine quality of the craftsmanship testifies to the high level of culture that Southeast China attained in the later part of the Chou period.

**11**   Ritual food container, *kuei*; bronze. Excavated in 1959 at T'un-hsi, Anhui Province. Late Western Chou or Early Eastern Chou, about eighth–early seventh century BC.
The semi-geometric decoration of this unique vessel is quite different from that on bronzes made in North China under the Chou, and suggests the influence of a local tradition of

stamped and impressed pottery decoration. At this time, this part of China was still in a very undeveloped state and the vessel, which combined fine craftsmanship with local features, was probably made for a ruling caste of Chou origin who had moved in from the Northwest.

12    Bovine creature, with a female standing on its back holding a revolving shaft supporting a flat openwork dish or offering stand; bronze. Ht. 15 cm., length 17.5 cm. From Ch'ang-chih, Shansi Province. Late Warring States period, fourth–third century BC.

It is not known what this strange object was meant for. Similar creatures bearing vessels on their backs are known in Chou bronze art; one with a flat openwork dish supported on a similar shaft was discovered in 1959 at Shan-piao-chen, Chi-hsien, Honan Province; but this combination of animal, dish-stand and human figure seems to be unique. It was excavated in 1965 from tomb No. 126 at Fen-shui-ling near Ch'ang-chih. The form of the animal and the decoration of its surface with scrolls, cloud bands, rope and cowrie shell patterns are in a style often called 'Li-yü' after a site in North Shansi where a group of bronzes was unearthed in 1923. But in the Warring States period the Ch'ang-chih region was much more important than Li-yü. Known as Shang-tang, it lay at the meeting point of the three states of Han, Yüeh and Wei, which had dismembered Chin in 376 BC. It remained a 'special area' under the Han, and was the home of many wealthy landowners until it was absorbed by the Ch'in unification of 230–221 BC. The lively form, rich decoration and fine finish of this piece proclaim it as a masterpiece of the bronze art created for the aristocracy of North China in the late Warring States period.

13    Creature with huge eyes, long lolling tongue and deer antlers, eating a snake; carved and lacquered wood. Ht. 195 cm. Excavated in 1957 from a tomb at Ch'ang-t'ai-kuan, in Hsin-yang-hsien, Honan Province. Late Warring States period, fourth–third century BC.

This is one of several similar objects that have been found in the area of Central China dominated by the culture of the State of Ch'u. It is not known whether they were meant as guardians, for worship, or for burial. Alfred Salmony suggested that the antlers and long tongue, which also adorn creatures painted on a calendrical document on silk from a Ch'u tomb at Changsha, were connected with ceremonies for bringing rain, but there is no proof of this. Whatever its function, this remarkable object is not only, like most of the objects from the waterlogged Ch'u tombs, very well preserved, but it illustrates magical beliefs and practices that seem to have been peculiar to the Ch'u people before they came under the dominating influence of the Northern Chinese civilization in the Han Dynasty.

**14–15**  Ritual vessel in the form of a rhinoceros; bronze, inlaid with gold. Length 57.8 cm. Found by a peasant in 1963 in an earthenware jar that had been buried in a deep pit near Tou-ma-ts'un, Hsing-p'ing-hsien, Shensi Province. Ch'in or Western Han Dynasty, third–second century BC.

This rhinoceros has a hinged lid on its back and holes in its snout, and is believed to have been used for pouring wine. Inside it were found a bronze openwork file, perhaps for massaging the skin, shells and other bronze and lacquer objects. The intricate inlaid decoration in no way robs this creature of its extraordinarily life-like quality. The rhinoceros was unknown in North China at this period, but so accurate is the modelling, down to the small beady eye of black and white glass paste, that the craftsman may have seen a living specimen in the imperial zoo where animals sent as gifts and as tribute were kept. The date of this beautiful piece is uncertain, but the area where it was found, just west of Sian, is rich in remains of the Ch'in and Western Han Dynasties.

The rhinoceros of mainland Asia has one horn, while the Sumatran and African species have two horns. It is extremely unlikely that an African rhinoceros could have reached North China, so we may assume that this one, and the famous two-horned Shang Dynasty specimen in the Brundage Collection in San Francisco, represent the Sumatran species, which at this time may have been found also on the mainland of Southeast Asia.

**16**  Mirror with three ring-handles; bronze, inlaid with gold, silver and turquoise. Diam. 29.8 cm. Excavated in 1963 at

Shang-wang-ts'un, Lin-tzu-hsien, Shantung Province. Late Chou period, fifth–third century BC.

This mirror is unusual for its large size and the ring handles for suspension instead of the usual central boss. The surface was polished, the reverse, shown here, being decorated with a geometrical design of which the bands end in volutes that suggest birds' heads. The vigorous swinging rhythm of this style is probably derived from lacquer painting. The decoration is also unusual, but there are bronze vases (*hu*) with rather similar motifs in the Pillsbury Collection in Minneapolis and the Freer Gallery in Washington.

Lin-tzu is the site of the capital of Ch'i of the Warring States period, and it is not unlikely that a mirror of this size and splendour was made for court use.

**17**    Covered square-section jar; lacquered wood. Ht. 50.5 cm. From a tomb at Ma-wang-tui, Changsha, Hunan Province, discovered late 1971. Western Han, about 180 BC.

This is one of the largest and most perfectly preserved Han lacquer vessels yet found. The decoration in horizontal bands consists chiefly of diagonals and volutes, or elaborate cloud scrolls picked out in two colours. While the shape of the vessel is copied from a bronze form (the *fang hu*), the style of the decoration is entirely natural to lacquer painting. Indeed, it was lacquer painting of this kind which provided the motifs and style of the decoration of many of the inlaid bronzes of the late Chou and Han.

**18–19**    Lady with Attendants. Detail of a hanging scroll; silk painted in mineral and vegetable colours. Total length of scroll 205 cm. Height of this detail, about 18 cm. From the tomb at Ma-wang-tui, Changsha, Hunan Province. Western Han Dynasty, about 180 BC.

This is a detail of the central section of a T-shaped silk scroll or banner, fitted with tassels and a cord for hanging, which was found draped over the body of the dead lady, believed to be the wife of Li Tsang, first Marquis of Ta, who was ennobled in 193 BC. The painting as a whole shows beings in the nether regions, in the world of man, and in the heavens. Most of the creatures are common in Han mythology and art, but this central part very likely depicts the

Marchioness herself, attended by servants or perhaps her daughters, receiving gifts from two kneeling youths. The detail is exquisitely painted, emphasis being given to the principal figure both by her size and by the splendid elaboration of her dress. Bolts of woven and embroidered silk with similar scroll designs were also found in the tomb, the contents of which, including the corpse itself, were in a remarkably fresh state of preservation.

This scroll is perhaps the most important single discovery in Chinese art in recent years. Clearly, from its fittings, it was not a funerary object but was meant to be hung on the wall and only later buried as a treasured possession of its owner. No authentic Chinese hanging scroll earlier than the Buddhist banners of the T'ang Dynasty from Tunhuang was previously known, so this discovery not only puts back the origin of this format by about a thousand years but also proves that the banner form was indigenous to China and not imported, as had been suggested, with Buddhist art from India after the Han Dynasty. As this painting is unique, there is no way of knowing whether the shape was common in the Han Dynasty, or was demanded by the subject-matter of this particular scroll.

**20–21**    Sacrificial Scene. Detail of the silk banner from the Ma-wang-tui tomb, Changsha, Hunan Province. About 180 BC.
This is near the bottom of the scroll. An atlantid with bulging muscles stands on giant fishes. Between his legs runs the body of a snake entwining the tails of two dragons who coil up the sides of the banner. The atlantid supports a platform on which an offering rite is being performed. In the foreground stand large, presumably bronze, vessels – *pien hu*, *hu*, and *ting* – and behind them the participants. Beyond stands an altar with yet more vessels, those on the left suggesting a stack of lacquer bowls with chopsticks such as were found in the tomb itself. The meaning of the decorated object in front of the altar is not clear. Above can be seen the lower edges of a V-shaped sonorous stone gong, while at the outer edges beyond the dragons' bodies are tortoises entwined with snakes. The tortoise and snake is a common symbol for the North in Han art, but the owls on their backs are unfamiliar visitors, perhaps peculiar to the local mythology of the State of Ch'u.

The artist's handling of depth in this scene is interesting, and more advanced than in the stone relief and engravings which have hitherto provided most of the evidence for Han pictorial art. The large vessels standing on the floor effectively throw the figures back into the middle ground and partly mask them, a device that early Chinese painters never, to our knowledge, attempted, while the small size of the vessels on the altar convincingly suggests the depth of the room. The fall of the participant's sleeves over the foreground vessels gives a charmingly natural touch.

22 Tray with five plates, one 'winged cup', *yü-shang*, two mugs, and a pair of chopsticks; lacquer. Length of tray 74.5 cm. From the tomb at Ma-wang-tui, Changsha, Hunan Province. Western Han Dynasty, about 180 BC.
The lacquer is chiefly wood-based, the decoration in black lacquer over red, with further touches added in red over the black. When found, the dishes still contained the cooked food set out over two thousand years ago, and there were many pairs of chopsticks. The typical Han 'winged cup', also made in bronze pottery, is generally considered as a wine cup, but inscriptions written inside the *yü-shang* in this tomb show that some were for food, ancestors of the rice bowl, others for wine.

While individual Han lacquer bowls and a few trays have found their way into Western collections, no set is known as perfect in condition and as complete as this one.

23 Model of a house; bronze. L. 73 cm. W. 42.7 cm. Ht. 37.3 cm. Excavated in 1971 from a tomb at Ho-pu, Kwangsi Province. Western Han Dynasty.
In Southeast Asia today timber or bamboo houses are generally built on piles, chiefly as protection against flooding. There is increasing evidence that this kind of construction, called *kan-lan* (pile dwellings), was once common in China south of the Yangtse River. Buildings on piles are shown on the top of some of the bronze cowrie-shell containers from Shih-chai-shan in Yünnan (plate 32), and in clay models found in Han tombs in the southern and western provinces of China, while a bronze coffin in the form of a longhouse on piles was unearthed in 1964 in

Hsiang-yün-hsien in Yünnan. The model illustrated here is further proof of the close links that existed between South China and Southeast Asia before the Han people penetrated this region and drew it into the orbit of Chinese culture.

**24–25**    Burial Suit; jade plaques, sewn together with gold thread. Length 188 cm. From the tomb of Liu Sheng, Prince Ching of Chung-shan, who died in 113 BC and was buried at Man-ch'eng, Hopei Province, about 140 km. southwest of Peking. His wife Tou Wan was buried near by. The concealed rock-cut tombs were discovered in 1968. Western Han Dynasty.

The Chinese believed that jade had the miraculous power of preventing the decay of the body, and from earliest times jade objects were set on and about the corpse. Jade suits, made only for members of the imperial family, show the extreme length to which this belief was carried in the Han Dynasty, after which the practice was abandoned.

'Jade clothes sewn with gold thread' are referred to in the *Han Shu* (History of the Han Dynasty) in descriptions of the burial of members of the imperial family, and the fragmented remains of a number of such suits have been found. In 1959, for example, over five thousand plaques of jade and white stone were found not far from Man-ch'eng, in a tomb believed to be that of Liu Yen, Prince of Chung-shan from AD 54 to 90. But this is the first time that such suits have been found sufficiently complete to be reconstructed.

Liu Sheng's suit is made of 2,498 thin plaques of jade, carefully varied in size and shape to secure a good fit. The plaques are drilled at the corners with tiny holes, some less than 0.5 mm. in diameter. The gold thread, totalling 1,110 grammes in weight, is beautifully made, some threads consisting of no less than twelve strands. Chinese authorities have calculated that it would take an expert craftsman ten years to make such a suit, and comment on the oppressive extravagance of China's feudal rulers.

**26**    Lamp; gilt bronze. Ht. 48 cm. From the tomb of Tou Wan, wife of Liu Sheng, who died in 113 BC. Western Han. This lamp, fitted with an adjustable shade, is held by a kneeling servant girl whose hollowed right arm acts as a chimney. There are several inscriptions engraved in the metal of the lamp; the longest, in 21 characters, refers to it as an 'eternal fidelity' (*ch'ang hsin*) lamp, and gives the oil capacity of the hollow body which was filled by removing the head. It was the custom in ancient China to inter oil lamps to lighten the eternal darkness of the tomb. Some of these were large basins of stone, such as the *wan-nien-teng*, 'ten thousand year lamp', found in the tomb of the tenth-century ruler Wang Chien in Chengtu; or of porcelain, such as were found in the tomb of the Wan-li Emperor of the Ming Dynasty. None, however, are as beautiful as the lamp from Tou Wan's tomb.

27 Covered wine vessel, *hu*; bronze, with gilded strapwork, silver studs, and glass inlay. Ht. 45 cm. From the tomb of Liu Sheng, 113 BC. Western Han Dynasty.
This handsome vessel has an inscription written inside which includes a name, Master Chen – perhaps the crafts-man who made it – and its capacity, five *tou* and five *sheng*.

A rather similar bronze *hu* inlaid with gold, silver and glass, in a Japanese collection, is believed to have come from Chin-ts'un near Loyang, where many fine inlaid bronzes of the late Warring States and Han have been found. The *hu* from the Liu Sheng tomb is more likely to have been made in the Loyang area than near Man-ch'eng itself, but there is no proof of this.

28 Double vessel, the two *tou* stem-cups being separated by a bird with a jade ring in its beak, standing on a tiger; gilt bronze, inlaid with silver and glass paste (?). Ht. 11.3 cm. From the tomb of Tou Wan. Western Han Dynasty, second century BC.
The function of this unique object has not been explained. It may have been a lamp.

29 *Po-shan hsiang-lu* (Fairy mountain incense burner); bronze, inlaid with gold. Ht. 26 cm. From the tomb of Liu Sheng (d. 113 BC) at Man-ch'eng, Hopei Province. Western Han Dynasty.
Po-shan is a mountain in Shantung Province. It is also the

name of a fairy mountain believed in Han mythology to be the dwelling place of Taoist immortals and fabulous beasts, and the source of the magic mushrooms which, if properly prepared, produce longevity. The smoke from incense burned inside the vessel drifting up from the holes in the lid behind the peaks suggested the *yün-ch'i*, cloud vapours, that showed that the mountain was 'alive and breathing', while the hunters pursuing their quarry suggested K'un-lun, the mountains of Central Asia and of many potent Han myths. The waves around the bowl denoted the Eastern Sea from which arises the unattainable fairy island of P'eng-lai.

Such hill-censers were given as wedding presents. It is not certain what their function was: references in early texts range from rites connected with mountain worship to the fumigating of bedding and clothing.

Another famous example of the *Po-shan hsiang-lu* is the inlaid and bejewelled censer in the Freer Gallery in Washington. The specimen we illustrate is less richly encrusted, but the combination of sweeping rhythmic form and precision of detail makes it the most perfect yet discovered.

**30–31** Tray with figures of acrobats, dancers, musicians and spectators or attendants; painted pottery. Length 67.5 cm.; width 47.5 cm. Excavated in 1969 from a tomb in a cemetery at Tsinan, Shantung Province. Western Han Dynasty, second–first century BC.

Among the twenty-one (originally twenty-two) figurines are four tumblers and two dancers in fancy dresses; percussion instruments include drums and stone chimes suspended from a frame; there are two *sheng* (bamboo pipes) and one *se* (zither). The grinning figure in the foreground is presumably the master of ceremonies.

The walls of Han tombs were often decorated with entertainment and feasting scenes to delight the spirit of the departed, and numbers of individual figurines of dancers, tumblers and musicians have been found. But this is the first time that a complete tableau of this kind has been discovered. It gives us a delightful picture of the sort of entertainment that was popular in Shantung in the Han Dynasty.

**32** Drum-shaped ritual container; bronze. Ht. 53 cm. From Shih-chai-shan, Chin-ning-hsien, Yünnan Province. Western Han Dynasty, second–first century BC.

While remains from the Chin-ning District have been known since World War II, the area was first excavated between 1955 and 1960, when more than thirty graves were opened on the rocky hillside of Shih-chai-shan. They yielded several drum-shaped containers crammed with cowrie-shells. The lids are crowded with figures cast in the round, depicting hunting, warfare or, as in this case, a sacrificial rite. Placed around the building on stilts are sixteen drums, while in front of it stands a large *ting*-type cauldron with a ladle across it. To the right are two gigantic drums. There is also a group of presumably sacrificial victims roped together, and several horses, not clearly visible in our reproduction.

The presence of Chinese artifacts such as a mirror in some of the later graves shows the influence of Han culture on these clearly non-Chinese people, who had no writing. Their links were much closer with the Bronze Age Dongson culture of Northern Indochina, while the type of building represented here suggests the Menangkabau longhouses of northern Sumatra. No drums as large as those represented here have been found in mainland Southeast Asia, but near Pedjeng on the island of Bali there is a bronze drum seven feet high and five feet across, of ancient Dongson type. How it reached Bali is a mystery.

**33** Two horsemen; painted pottery. Ht. 68 cm. and 65 cm. Found in 1965 at Yang-chia-wan near Shen-yang, Shensi Province. Western Han Dynasty.

Both the riders and their horses are painted, their costumes, armour and hairstyle being clearly shown; and most of the horses have a number scratched on their flanks. The upper part of the horsemen and the horses' tails were made separately. These are among 580 horsemen and 2,000 human figures that were found standing in closely packed rows, in six separate pits. The tomb with which they were associated has not been discovered, although across a stream to the north are two burial mounds.

The tomb of the Han Emperor Kao Tzu (206–194 BC) is four kilometres away, and it is possible that these pits might have been connected with the tomb of one of his high officials. The burial of the figurines near the tomb derives from the Shang custom of interring slaughtered slaves and horses in separate pits, as seen at Anyang.

**34—35**  Pacing horse, with one hoof resting on a flying swallow; bronze. Length 45 cm. From Lei-t'ai, Wu-wei-hsien, Kansu Province. Late Eastern Han, second century AD.

This beautiful piece was unearthed in 1969 from a very large tomb that had already been robbed in ancient times. Among over 220 objects left behind by the robbers were 14 bronze chariots, 17 bronze horses and riders, 45 figurines of chariot drivers, escorts, male and female servants, and this piece, which vividly expresses the almost divine qualities that the horse was believed in the eyes of the Han people to possess. While no comparable Han bronzes have been discovered before, the horses bear some resemblance in style to the pottery horses with riders discovered in 1957 in Han graves at T'ien-hui-shan outside Chengtu in Szechwan, and suggest that the vigorous culture of Shu, as Szechwan was called in ancient times, may have influenced the makers of the bronzes in the Lei-t'ai tomb.

**36**  Case for an inkstone in the form of a mythical monster; gilt bronze, inlaid with silver, coral and turquoise. Length about 22 cm. From Hsü-chou, Kiangsu Province. Eastern Han Dynasty.

This beautiful object, excavated with other treasures in 1969 from an undisturbed tomb, hinges open to reveal the inkstone, the top half then forming a water receptacle or brush-washer. The fact that the corpse was clothed in a jade burial suit sewn with silver thread has led Chinese authorities to suggest that this may be the tomb of Liu Kung, Prince of P'eng-ch'eng, son of the later Han Emperor Ming (r. 58—76).

**37**  Detail of a lacquered wooden screen panel. Ht. of one section about 20 cm. From the tomb of Ssu-ma Chin-lung, who was buried in 484 at Tatung, Shansi Province. Northern Wei Dynasty.

Ssu-ma Chin-lung, who claimed descent from the famous Han scholar Ssu-ma T'an, was a high official who served the Northern Wei with such distinction that he was granted burial in the imperial mausoleum, Chin-ling. The tomb, which had been robbed long ago, was excavated in 1965–66. The screen panels were found standing against the wall of the inner chamber of the tomb. The upper scene, in which a lady kneels before another seated on a dais, has not been positively identified. Below, we see an incident recorded in the *Lieh Nü Chuan*, Biographies of Virtuous Women, when the imperial concubine Pan refused to go out with the Emperor Ch'eng (32–5 BC) in his palanquin; she told him it was more fitting that he take with him one of his ministers and devote the outing to discussion of affairs of state. The emperor looks back appealingly, but the Lady Pan, standing on the right, is not to be persuaded. The labels give the names of the protagonists and tell the story.

Apart from wall paintings – chiefly Buddhist – practically no examples of Six Dynasties painting are known, and this is a discovery of major importance. The bright red background must have been fashionable at the time, for it also appears in fifth century wall paintings at Tunhuang, where it has been, erroneously perhaps, ascribed to Near Eastern influence. There is nothing foreign about these pictures. Not only are the theme and style completely Chinese, but the treatment of the Lady Pan scene almost exactly duplicates that in the famous scroll of the Admonitions of the Court Instructress, in the British Museum, attributed to Ku K'ai-chih (c. 340–406). Whether Ku K'ai-chih originated this treatment, or both derive from an even earlier rendering, is not known. But the appearance of such similar compositions, one far to the north in Wei-controlled territory, the other stemming from the Nanking artist Ku K'ai-chih seven hundred miles to the south in 'Free China', suggests that by the late fifth century the foreign occupation of half China was no barrier to the transmission of artistic conventions. The screen may even have been painted by an artist trained in the south.

Only in one significant point do the two versions differ. Ku K'ai-chih (if the scroll in the British Museum is his work, or a copy of it) has with ironic humour put another young lady in the palanquin beside the Emperor, giving added point to Lady Pan's protest.

38    Stem cup, decorated round below the rim with seven animals in appliqué relief confronting each other (an eighth is missing), and on the body with Hellenistic figures and four heads, the space between them having acanthus scrolls in low relief; gilt bronze. Ht. 10.3 cm. From the tomb of Ssu-ma Chin-lung (died AD 484), Tatung, Shansi Province. Northern Wei Dynasty.

The shape and decoration of this wine cup are Western Asiatic in origin. Remarkably similar relief decoration appears around the upper part of an ivory rhyton discovered in the ruins of the Parthian city of Nisa in Turkmenistan, destroyed by an earthquake in 454. If indeed this piece was made in China, the craftsmen were very probably foreigners from Central Asia or even further west.

39    Flask, decorated with dancer and musicians in relief under a golden-brown glaze; stoneware. Ht. 19.5 cm. From the tomb of Fan Tsui (died 575), governor of Liangchou under the Northern Ch'i Dynasty. Excavated at Anyang, Honan Province, in 1971.

The shape of this vessel, the decoration, and the style and dress of the figures are all Central Asian, thoroughly influenced by Sassanian art. The vessel, however, was made by Chinese potters, presumably in local kilns in northern Honan or southern Shansi. It shows that the taste in ceramics for exotic Western shapes and styles among the Chinese gentry, thought typical of the T'ang, was already well-established in North China in the sixth century.

40–41  Worshippers or donors in the lower left corner of a panel of silk embroidery, of which the main central part is missing. Excavated in 1965 from the ground in front of Caves 125–126 at Tunhuang, Kansu Province. Northern Wei Dynasty. The five figures, reading from right to left, are the presumed donor Yüan-chia, or Prince of K'uang-yang, his mother, his wife, and two other female members of the family. Their Buddhist names are in cartouches to the right of each figure. At the extreme right can be seen the last line of the votive inscription; the date is obliterated but has been established from internal evidence as equivalent to 487. In the upper part of the picture the lotus thrones of a principal Buddha (right) and a standing subsidiary figure can be seen, suggesting a composition very similar to that of a wall-painting in Cave 251 at Tunhuang. The style of the costumes is quite un-Chinese, and resembles Toba Turkish dress as depicted in a relief in Cave II at Yünkang, the cave-temples near the Wei capital of P'ing-ch'eng (modern Tatung). There is no evidence that K'uang-yang Wang was ever at Tunhuang, and Chinese authorities suggest that this panel might have been made at P'ing-ch'eng and brought to Tunhuang by a traveller.

42  Vase; slipped and splashed with green under a crackled white glaze. Ht. 23 cm. Stoneware. From the tomb of Fan Tsui (d. 575) at Anyang, Honan Province. North Ch'i Dynasty.
This masterpiece of the Chinese potter's art is an example of a type of pottery with coloured glazes which, until its discovery, was thought to have been characteristic of the seventh rather than the sixth century in North China.

43  Jar; stoneware slipped and glazed in yellow splashed with green, with four lugs and a design of floral scrolls and lotus leaves incised in the clay under the glaze. Ht. about 22 cm. Excavated from a tomb at Pu-yang, Honan Province. Northern Ch'i Dynasty (550–77).
The discovery of this vessel, like that in the previous plate, shows that the robust contours and polychrome glazes which have been thought to have originated in the Sui Dynasty at the earliest, were already developed in the Northern Ch'i period. The simplified acanthus scrolls and lotus leaves proclaim the influence of Western Asiatic and Buddhist art in North China at this time.

44  Seated woman; glazed pottery. From a tomb at Loyang, Honan Province. T'ang Dynasty, eighth century.
This is a fine example of the dignified yet lively tomb figurines made at the height of T'ang prosperity.

45 Saddled and bridled horse; pottery glazed in black, brown and green. Ht. 66.8 cm. Discovered in 1970 in Tomb No. 120 at Kuan-lin, Loyang, Honan Province. T'ang Dynasty.

This animal is exceptional both for its large size and for the black glaze that covers the body, which is very rare in T'ang ceramics.

46 Camel bearing on his back a troupe of musicians; glazed pottery. Ht. 48.5 cm. Excavated in 1959 near Sian, Shensi Province. T'ang Dynasty.

Of the camels with musicians on their backs that have turned up since 1949 during construction work and excavation in Sian, this is the most elaborate. The singing girl is surrounded by men playing a variety of instruments including the straight flute (*ti*), clappers, *sheng* (a kind of bamboo organ) and lute (*p'i-p'a*). They sit on a thick wool carpet of Central Asian type, but the figures themselves, unlike the musicians on some of the other camels, appear to be Chinese. The potter, obviously trying to see how many people he could put on the camel's back, has shrunk them to child size, but their animation makes them entirely believable.

Until recently it was thought that the three-colour glazed figurines first appeared in the reign of the 'empress' Wu (683–705), but the discovery of such figures in the tomb of General Cheng Jen-t'ai (d. 663/4) shows that they were being made at least twenty years earlier, so these may be dated between 660 and 760, after which the use of polychrome glazed figures declined sharply.

47 Rhyton; carved onyx with gold tip to the muzzle. Length 15.5 cm. Unearthed at Ho-chia-ts'un, Sian, Shensi Province, in 1970. T'ang Dynasty.

The Ho-chia-ts'un hoard consists of over 1,000 pieces, including many superb examples of gold and silverware, which had been carefully packed and buried in the grounds of the mansion that had belonged to the Prince of Pin (d. 741). His son is believed to have buried these treasures before fleeing to Szechwan with the Emperor Hsüan Tsung when the rebel General An Lu-shan attacked Ch'ang-an in 756. If so, their owner never returned to claim them.

Rhytons, copying a form of drinking cup that is ultimately of Mesopotamian origin, appear in the crafts of the Six Dynasties and T'ang, generally in stoneware or porcelain, more rarely in metalwork. Chinese authorities believe that this unique and beautiful piece was made in Central Asia, where rhytons were used by the Uighurs and other non-Chinese peoples, although a Chinese origin for it cannot be ruled out.

**48** Flask; silver, with gilt repoussé decoration of a horse with a wine-cup in its mouth. Ht. 14.5 cm. From the Ho-chia-ts'un hoard, Sian, Shensi Province. T'ang Dynasty, eighth century.

The shape of this vessel is copied from the skin wine-flask carried by the Turkic peoples of Central Asia, while the technique is Sassanian. The origin of the horse with a wine cup in its mouth is harder to establish. It does not occur in Sassanian art. In the Six Dynasties and T'ang, however, water-droppers for mixing ink on the scholar's desk were sometimes made, in metal or jade, in the form of a crouching mythical beast holding a wine cup in its mouth. But there may be a more interesting and amusing explanation. The T'ang emperor Ming-huang, who had a passion for horses, was said to own four hundred horses specially trained to dance and to bring winecups in their mouths and lay them before the emperor's feet at imperial banquets. A verse by the T'ang poet Chang Shuo describing this extraordinary spectacle says that in the process the horses became 'as drunk as mud' (*tsui ju ni*) – which would explain the position this animal has assumed.

**49** Covered jar with swing handle, decorated with parrots encircled by peony sprays with floral ornament on foot, neck and lid; beaten silver with traced decoration in gilt. Ht. 24.2 cm. Inside the lid is an inscription giving the contents as follows: 'amethyst (*tz'u-ying*), fifty ounces; quartz (*pa'i-ying*), twelve ounces'. From the Ho-chia-ts'un hoard, Sian, Shensi Province. T'ang Dynasty, eighth century.

In design and craftsmanship this vessel is the equal of those preserved in the Shōsōin Repository at Nara in Japan, and a good example of the splendour of decorative art at the climax of T'ang prosperity.

50 Eight-sided wine cup; in each panel a figure of a dancer, musician or man offering a bowl(?) against a background of flowers and birds; on the ring handle two old men's heads with deep-set eyes and high noses, and long hair hanging down; gilt bronze. Ht. 6.5 cm. From the Ho-chiats'un hoard, Sian, Shensi Province. T'ang Dynasty.

The eight-sided cup with ring-handle and thumb-piece is common in Sassanian metalwork, but rare in China; there are T'ang examples in the Kempe and Erickson Collections. In T'ang examples, the classical figures are replaced by an all-over floral pattern – an instance of the T'ang 'sinicization' of forms first introduced into China in the fifth and sixth centuries.

51 Weft-pattern polychrome silk; decorated in five colours with phoenixes, flowers and other plants on a red background. Found in 1966 in a tomb dated 778 in the Astana cemetery near Turfan, Sinkiang Province. T'ang Dynasty, eighth century.

This fine example of silk weaving belongs to the mature T'ang period, when the formal Sassanian elements have been absorbed into a sumptuous floral design that is entirely Chinese in flavour.

52 Inkstone in the form of a pool bordered by a fairy mountain; on the mountain are the magic mushrooms of immortality, *ling-chih*, a suggestion of verdure and several birds; glazed pottery. Ht. not given, but probably about 20 cm. Excavated at Sian, Shensi Province. T'ang Dynasty.

Inkstones, or tablets for grinding ink, were made in a wide variety of materials and forms. This is not the only T'ang example flanked by fairy mountains, but it seems to be unique in its lively modelling, its birds, and the beauty of its glaze. While Chinese authorities call it an inkstone, and ink could certainly be ground on its unglazed base, it may also have been used as a brush-washer.

**53** Vase, decorated with formalized flower patterns impressed under a warm reddish-brown glaze; the body is fitted on each side with lugs, channels, and holes in the foot to hold a strap; stoneware. Ht. not given, but probably about 25–30 cm. Excavated in 1960 at Ho-lin-ko, Mongolia, formerly Suiyuan Province, about 120 km. west of Tatung. Late T'ang or tenth century.

This vessel and the succeeding one were found in a group of brick tombs, presumably of Mongol chieftains. Vessels like this slung from the saddle are represented in T'ang grave figurines of camels. It is not known where or precisely when this handsome vessel was made, but it was evidently produced in North China under the late T'ang or succeeding Liao Dynasty for the use of China's nomadic northern neighbours.

**54** Ewer in the shape of a parrot, covered with a green and yellow glaze; stoneware. Ht. 19.5 cm. Discovered in 1960 in a tomb at Ho-lin-ko, Mongolia. Late T'ang or tenth century.

Like the preceding vessel, almost certainly made in North China under Late T'ang or Liao. There is nothing in the shape and decoration of this piece, however, to suggest that it was not made for the domestic market. A very similar parrot, covered with a warm yellow glaze, was found in 1969 in a tomb dated 977 at Ting-chou in Hopei.

**55** Box for sûtras or relics; polychrome-glazed pottery. From Mi-hsien, Honan Province. Sung Dynasty.

The box is in the form of a treasury with guardians flanking the doors and watchdogs at the corners, and the 'roof' forming the lid. The walls and roof are stamped with floral rosettes and scrolls. The shape of the box as a whole is probably copied from metalwork, but the stamped floral rosettes and scrolls that decorate the surface, and the streaked polychrome glazes, retain a good deal of the flavour of T'ang ceramics. This spectacular object suggests a possible Northern Sung date for other polychrome glazed pieces which we are apt to give to the Liao Dynasty, or to the T'ang.

**56**    Vase, with lotus leaves incised under a celadon glaze; Yo-yao stoneware, Ht. 33.5 cm. Excavated in Changsha in 1958. Five Dynasties period, 906–60.

This lovely vase is a good example of the rather thinly glazed celadon that was produced at the Yo-chou kilns in Hunan between the T'ang and the Sung. It is now in the Hunan Provincial Museum, Changsha.

**57**    Vase, decorated with peonies carved through a white glaze to a brownish slip; stoneware. Ht. not given. From T'ang-yin-hsien, Hopei Province. Sung Dynasty.

This is a type of ware known to have been made in the group of villages around Hao-pi, in T'ang-yin-hsien, south of Anyang. Four kiln-sites were discovered here in 1952 and investigated two years later. They made a great variety of monochrome and decorated stonewares, of which this vase is a particularly lovely example.

**58**    Fragment of a lacquer dish inlaid with mother-of-pearl. Length 20 cm. Discovered in 1970 at the site of a Yüan gentleman's mansion at Hou-ying-fang, Peking. Yüan Dynasty.

The design on this fragment is thought to show the Kuang-han-kung, the Palace of Cold Vastness on the Moon, to which, according to legend, the fairy Ch'ang-o escaped. Several pieces of lacquer inlaid with mother-of-pearl have been dated to the fourteenth century on grounds of style, including a tray with dragon design in the Tokyo National Museum, and a box in the S. Y. Lee Collection containing writing sets which may have been made for the Mongol court. But until the excavation of this piece, no lacquer inlaid with mother-of-pearl could be dated to the Yüan with absolute certainty.

**59**    Flask with spout in the form of a phoenix head, decorated in cobalt blue under the glaze; porcelain. Ht. 18.5 cm. Yüan Dynasty.

This broken and restored flask is one of the cache of sixteen pieces of porcelain, covered with a pottery basin, which was discovered in Peking in 1970 in the ruins of a gentleman's mansion near the city wall at Old Drum Tower Street, Chiu-ku-lou Ta Kai. It is believed that they may have been hastily buried during the troubles that accompanied the fall of the Mongol Yüan Dynasty in 1368.

While there is ample documentary and circumstantial evidence for blue and white porcelain in the Yüan Dynasty, and a few pieces bearing Yüan dates are known – notably the famous pair of vases dated 1351 in the Percival David Foundation in London – very few pieces have been excavated from known Yüan sites. This fact, and the very unusual shape of this delightful vessel, give it a unique importance in the history of Chinese ceramics.

60 Kuan-yin (Goddess of Mercy); white porcelain (*ch'ing-pai* or *ying-ch'ing* ware). Ht. 25 cm. From the ruins of the Yüan capital Ta-tu (Peking). Yüan Dynasty.
Combining sweetness and dignity, this is an exquisite example of the porcelain sculpture, chiefly of Buddhist figures, produced at the Ching-te-chen kilns in the Yüan Dynasty. The delicately detailed ropes of beads are typical of the period.

61 Dish in the form of a flower, the petals resembling the auspicious sceptre (*ju-i*) or cloud-collar (*yün-ling*); gold decorated with chased floral ornament. 16 cm. square. Discovered in 1959 at Tiger Hill, Soochow, Kiangsu Province, in the richly-furnished tomb of Lü Shih-meng, who died in 1304, and his wife, who died in 1315. Yüan Dynasty.
A fine example of Yüan goldsmiths' work, particularly valuable because, unlike so much supposedly Yüan metalwork, it is securely dated.

62 Wine-jar decorated with floral designs emerging from rockwork, set in ogival open-work panels surrounded by a double band of pearl beading; round the shoulder are *ju-i*-shaped panels containing flowers amid waves alternating with peonies. The neck has a band of chrysanthemum scrolls and there are lotus leaf panels with flowers around the foot. Lotus panels also adorn the lid which has a knob

in the form of a lion-dog; porcelain, decorated in underglaze blue and red. Yüan Dynasty.

This is one of a group of vessels, chiefly blue and white, unearthed by construction workers building a primary school at Pao-ting in Shensi Province. It is a magnificent example of a type of wine-jar combining openwork panels and underglaze red and blue glaze, of which a specimen, which had been used by its English owners for many years as an umbrella-stand, was sold, without a cover, in London in June 1972 for the record price of 210,000 guineas. The Pao-ting jar is especially rare in that the cover has survived intact.

63     Incense-burner; stoneware decorated with three-colour glazes. Ht. 36 cm.

The open-work decoration consists of phoenixes amid flowers on the body, a band of lotus flowers around the neck, and a cloud-band round the collar. The lid is in the form of a fairy mountain, *Po-shan*, adorned with dragons, rising out of the waves. Excavated in 1964 from a disused well in the Hai-tien district of Peking, beneath the early Ming city wall. Although no inscription has yet been published, the Yüan date may be on one of the handles or the rim.

This type of glazed pottery (*liu-li*) was made in Shansi Province from the Yüan Dynasty onwards, being used also for relief sculpture, ridge tiles, and the facing of pagodas. Some years ago the Chinese ceramics expert Ch'en Wan-li found in Shansi a similar *ting* bearing the date 1308 and the maker's name, Master Ch'iao. He also found in Peking *liu-li* animals bearing Ming (1603) and Ch'ing (1649) dates. The tradition seems to have been handed down in certain families in several cities of Shansi.

While the lid of this piece is a grotesque parody of the ancient hill censer (plate 29), the ungainly shape, bold modelling and crude colour are just what one imagines the Mongol rulers and their Central Asiatic henchmen would have regarded as fitting adornment for their palaces and mansions.

**64**    Eight-sided dish; porcelain. It is decorated in five-colour, *wu-ts'ai*, enamels with figures in a landscape, more figures in landscapes round the rim, and flowers in the panels on the outside. Diam. 36.7 cm. Six character mark of Wan-li (1573–1620). Late Ming Dynasty.

This dish was discovered in 1964 in a Ch'ing Dynasty chamber for cremated ashes at Ta-t'un-ts'un, outside the An-ting Gate of Peking. The latest objects in the chamber were coins of the K'ang-hsi period (1666–1722), which provide a date for the burial. The scene in the centre, more simply repeated in the smaller panels, depicts the famous fourth-century calligrapher Wang Hsi-chih admiring geese, of which he was extremely fond. Perhaps the two servants are bringing him the geese that were offered by a Taoist priest in exchange for Wang's having written out for him the text of the *Tao Te Ching*.

## A Note on Sources

The works of art illustrated here were for the most part originally published in Chinese books and periodicals, such as: *Wen-wu Ta Ko-ming ch'i-chien ch'u-t'u wen-wu*, Cultural Relics Unearthed during the Great Cultural Revolution (Peking, 1972), and *Hsin Chung-kuo ch'u-t'u wen-wu*, Historical Relics Unearthed in New China (Peking, 1972), and in the archaeological journals *Wen Wu* and *Kaogu*. In a few cases the dimensions have not been published. The photographs on pages 23 and 30 were taken by Dominique Darbois. The picture of the Changsha wood carving (Plate 13) appeared in Akiyama Terukazu and Others, *Arts of China* Vol. I (Tokyo and Palo Alto, 1968); our thanks are due to Kodansha International for permission to publish.

Readers who would like a fuller treatment of Chinese art than is given in the introductory section of this book are referred to my *Short History of Chinese Art* (1967), of which a new edition, incorporating much of the recently discovered material, will shortly be published by Thames and Hudson.

M.S.

2

3

4

5

10

14–15

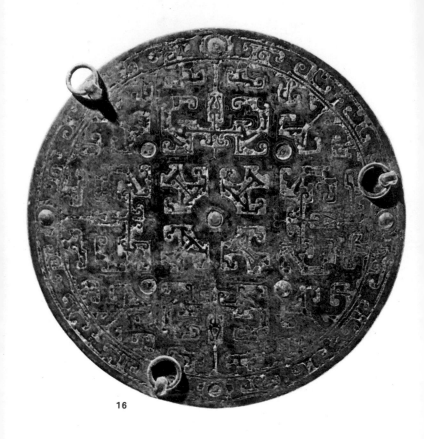

16

23

24—25

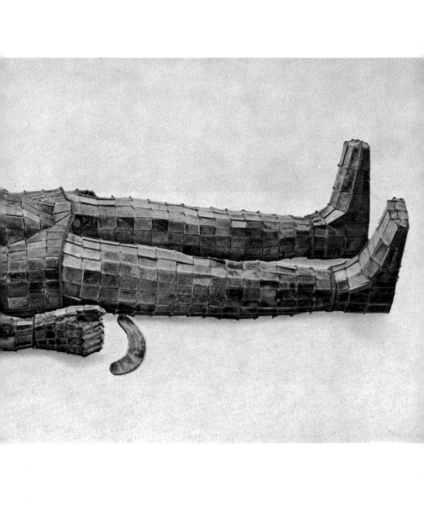

33

36

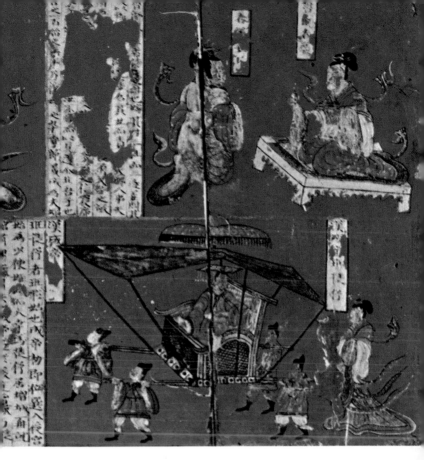

37

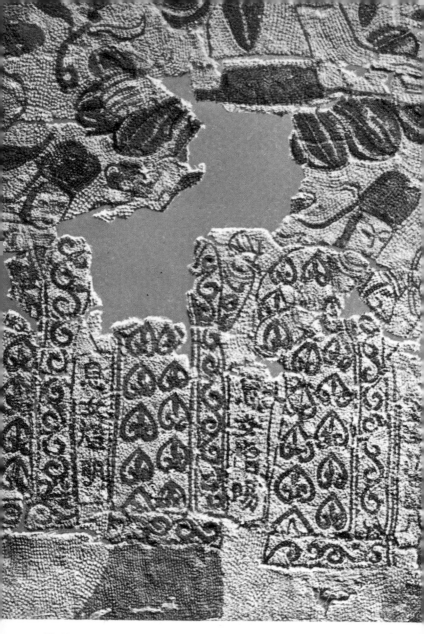

46

49

50

51

58

59

60          61

**64**